Bill Fletcher

Great Scottish Feats of Engineering and Building

Illustrated by John Marshall

Richard Drew Publishing, Glasgow

British Library Cataloguing in Publication Data
Fletcher, William
Great Scottish feats of engineering. — (Otter books)
1. Engineering — Scotland — History — Juvenile literature
I. Title   II. Series
620'.009411   TA61
ISBN 0-86267-118-3
ISBN 0-86267-117-5 Pbk

First Published 1986 by Richard Drew Publishing Ltd
6 Clairmont Gardens, Glasgow G3 7LW

Copyright © 1986 Bill Fletcher

Designed by James W Murray
Printed and bound in Great Britain
Set in Raleigh by John Swain Ltd, Glasgow

Roads for the Highlands

In 1725 General George Wade was made Commander-in-Chief of Scotland by the British Government. His job was to subdue the Highland clans and in order to do this he built roads along which his troops and horses and cannon could move. Between the years 1726 and 1740, he built 243 miles (390 km) of roads and 40 bridges, linking up Fort William, Fort Augustus and Fort George and also penetrating into the Highlands. The roads consisted of large stones laid at the bottom of a trench, followed by smaller stones, then gravel beaten hard by shovels.

These roads were, however, of little use to the Highlanders. For centuries the mainstay of Highland economy was cattle which were grazed on common land. In the meantime, people in the Lowlands were becoming more prosperous due to increased employment and production as a result of the Industrial Revolution and this was leading to a growing demand for beef. The Highlanders took their cattle 'on the hoof' from the glens to the markets of the south. But they didn't use General Wade's roads. They took them along the old 'drove roads' which were little more than tracks through the mountains.

That way of life was soon to cease. Bonnie Prince Charlie's Highland Army was defeated by Government troops at Culloden Moor in 1746. The commander of the victorious army – the Duke of Cumberland — showed no mercy. The wounded were shot as they lay and the Government troops were sent out into the countryside to burn the houses, hunt out the clans and destroy them. The Highlands became a wilderness. Many people emigrated to Canada and America.

The British Government became very worried about this depopulation, which they had helped to create, and in 1801 they asked Thomas Telford to make a report. Telford has been described as Britain's greatest civil engineer. He was born, the son of a poor shepherd, near Langholm in Dumfriesshire in 1757. His father died while Thomas was still a baby, but a relative paid for him to attend the local school until he was fourteen. He became a stonemason. When he went to London his true worth was appreciated and in time he was appointed a county surveyor. He supervised the building of the great Ellesmere Canal to link up the Rivers Mersey, Dee and Severn. He built many bridges. He was recognised as being a brilliant engineer. He made two surveys of

Thomas Telford was also responsible for building the Caledonian Canal (see p.4) and the London to Holyhead road, in the course of which he built the magnificent suspension bridges at Menai and at Conway in Wales. He built the Bridge over the Water of Leith, Edinburgh and the Broomielaw Bridge in Glasgow. He was responsible also for the Gotha Canal giving Sweden a water-way from the Baltic to the North Sea. He was the first President of the Institution of Civil Engineers. When he died in 1874 he was buried in Westminster Abbey.

the Highlands, on one of which he went on a four months' journey, and in these he emphasised that the great need was for roads so that trade would develop. There was also a great need for work for Highlanders. He reported that 3000 had left in 1801 and 9000 were expected to leave in 1802. The Government were very impressed with his report and told him to proceed with his plans.

So over the next eighteen years Telford was responsible for planning, designing and building 1200 bridges in Scotland, including very important ones over the Rivers Tay, Dee and Spey and over the Dornoch Firth. He also built 920 miles (1500 km) of new roads and renewed 280 miles (450 km) of military roads. He built a short ferry connecting with a road that ran the entire length of the Isle of Skye. He also built 42 churches in the Highlands and he carried out improvements on the harbours of Aberdeen, Banff, Cullen, Dundee, Fraserburgh, Peterhead and Dingwall. He completely transformed the Highlands. By 1820 there was a regular service of forty coaches a week between Perth and Inverness. Carts replaced pack-horses and a great trade in raw materials and manufactured goods built up between the Highlands and the Lowlands. But Telford took the greatest pride in that not only did he supply work for the Highlanders, but he taught them *how* to work. He employed more than 3000 men each year. They learned skills and abilities which they later took back to their native villages.

In the Highlands Telford used a method of road building that went back to the Romans. After levelling and draining, he made a base of large pavement stones. They were then covered with a layer of smaller stones about the size of walnuts. A thin layer of gravel was laid on top.

Forth and Clyde, Crinan and Caledonian Canals

Five years before the Forth and Clyde Canal was completed, Robert Whitworth took over as Chief Engineer. One of his greatest feats in building the Canal was the construction of a great aqueduct over the River Kelvin. It was more than 400 ft (120 metres) in length. Spectators could look up from the ground below and see a vessel sailing past 70 ft (20 metres) over their heads.

In 1763 a group with the imposing title of 'The Board of Trustees for the Encouragement of Fisheries, Manufactures and Improvements in Scotland' asked John Smeaton, a Yorkshire engineer, to build a canal to link up the Firth of Clyde with the Firth of Forth, so that goods could be shipped right across Scotland.

Water to the canal was supplied by neighbouring rivers such as the Kelvin, the Calder and the Luggie Burn and in some cases great reservoirs, such as that at Townhead in Glasgow which covered 70 acres (28 hectares), were constructed. Others were built in the Monklands. Building the canal was hard, dangerous work through heavy wet clay, often in foul weather. There were many accidents and many men fell ill with fever. Not surprisingly, the Company made an arrangement with the nearby Glasgow Royal Infirmary that their sick would be admitted without the signature of a parish minister.

The canal was completed in 1790. It stretched 35 miles (56 km) from the little town of Bowling on the River Clyde to Grangemouth on the River Forth. There were a number of branches, the most important being the one into Port Dundas in the heart of Glasgow, where a great basin covering eight acres (three hectares) was created. Edinburgh had no connection, but later the Edinburgh and Union Canal was built to link up with the Forth and Clyde Canal at Falkirk.

The summit of the Canal was at the lock at Castlecary which was 156 feet (47 metres) above sea level, with twenty locks between it and Grangemouth and nineteen locks between it and Bowling. Fishing boats sailed through from the west to fish for herring in the Firth of Forth. But the main traffic on the Canal was barges carrying grain, flour, salt, sugar, timber, coal, iron, slates and other goods; and the great value of the Canal to the people of the west of Scotland was shown when grain shipped from Europe helped to avert a famine.

When the Monkland Canal was built by James Watt in 1793 it brought coal from the Monklands twelve miles (nineteen kilometres) away, to Glasgow. Barges on the Canal were pulled by horses which were changed regularly on the way and it was a rule that the canals be

closed in winter when the ice got so thick that it took more than ten horses to pull a single boat.

The first attempt to replace horse power by steam power was in 1803. William Symington (who invented the world's first steam boat) fitted engines to drive the paddles on the 'Charlotte Dundas' on the Forth and Clyde Canal. Although the trial was a great success, the Governors of the Canal forbade any further trials as they said that the waves from the paddles were washing away the canal banks. It was not until many years later that steam was used again. By then, however, the canal trade was beginning to suffer because of competition from the developing railways. And there were other worries. Even as early as 1836 the Reverend Andrew Sym of Kilpatrick near Glasgow was complaining that funeral expenses of people drowned in the Canal seriously reduced his parish funds! The Forth and Clyde Canal was closed in 1961. The closure of the Union Canal followed in 1963. The Monkland Canal was abandoned in 1950 and has now been filled in.

The Crinan Canal stretches from Lochgilphead on Loch Fyne to Crinan on the Sound of Jura. It was built so that trade could be easily opened up between the Western Isles without sailing ships having to make the long and dangerous sea journey round the Mull of Kintyre.

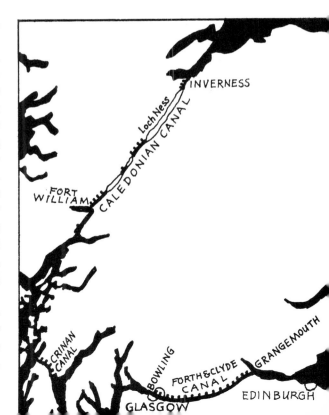

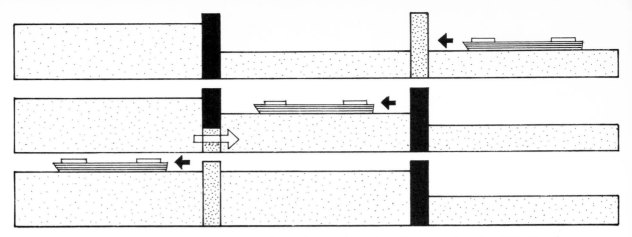

Canal locks were invented in the 14th century. Until then, canals could only be built on level ground. A lock is a device for raising or lowering a boat from one level of the canal to another. It consists of a huge basin of water with flood-gates at each end. When the barge (or boat) is going upstream, the lower gate is opened and the barge sails into the basin. The lower gate is then closed. Vents in the upper gate are opened and water floods in, raising the barge to the upper level. The process is reversed when the barge is going downstream.

Work was begun in 1793 and soon six hundred Highlanders were at work with their picks, shovels and barrows. But these tools were not much use when they met solid rock, which had to be blasted away. Building materials were brought in from the islands of Arran, Bute, Jura, Mull, Colonsay and others. Because of the difficulties and expense the Company began to run out of money. The Canal was opened in a very unfinished state in 1801 and the real difficulties had only really begun. Some vessels could not use it because the water was not deep enough. Most of the timber for the drawbridges and locks was American oak and soon it began to rot. Part of the canal banks were washed away by floods. The banks of one of the big reservoirs collapsed; water rushed into the Canal and two locks were swept away. The Company applied for financial help to the Government who, while giving it, insisted that control should be handed over to the Commissioners of the Caledonian Canal; Thomas Telford, the famous engineer, was appointed to take charge of repairs. He practically rebuilt the Canal, extending the pier at Ardrishaig, deepening the eastern entrance, replacing the wooden drawbridges with cast-iron ones, renewing the lock gates, widening and straightening the Canal in parts.

The Canal was re-opened in 1817; it proved a great boon to trading and travel to and from the Western Isles. Sailing boats carried passengers and goods and following the success of the 'Comet' the first European steamboat, in 1812 steam soon replaced sail. Among the goods carried were sheep, pigs, cattle, boxes and barrels of herring, coal, slates, building stones and whisky, all for the great markets of Glasgow. Passenger steamers carried holidaymakers out to the Isles.

Again, however, the coming of the railways reduced the importance of the Canal. Although now more sailing boats than ever go through the Canal, they are pleasure yachts.

The Caledonian Canal runs from Inverness to Fort William and thus joins up the North Sea and the Atlantic Ocean. By using it, ships can avoid the long and sometimes dangerous passage around the stormy seas of the north of Scotland. It is one of the most beautiful waterways in the world, going through the heart of Scotland's Great Glen and from it one can get a wonderful view of Britain's highest mountain – Ben Nevis. Although the passage is 60 miles (96 km) long, only 22 miles (35 km) of it is man-made, joining up the remaining 38 miles (61 km) of natural deep water lochs – Loch Ness (of monster fame), Loch Oich (which is the highest point) and Loch Lochy. There are 29 locks. It was Thomas Telford who proposed such a canal in 1801, though James Watt had suggested it thirty years earlier. The idea was adopted by the Government and Thomas Telford was put in charge.

Turf houses were built for the workmen and workshops for the blacksmiths and carpenters. The best timbers were brought from Aberdeen, as well as railways and wagons, by boat. Three Boulton and Watt steam engines from Birmingham were used to pump out water during the building of locks and in the deepening of lochs. Cast-iron swing bridges were built. Stones were brought from Lismore, from the Cumbrae islands on the Clyde and from the Black Isle. The scene at the construction of a lock at Loch Ness is vivid. 'Men, horses and machines were at work digging, walling and puddling. Men wheeling barrows, horses drawing stones along the roadway. The great steam engine was at rest having done its work, but the dredging machine was in action, revolving round and round, bringing up at every turn matter which had never before been brought to the air and light'.

The Canal, which has been described as 'one of the most stupendous undertakings of that nature which Europe has seen', was opened in 1822, amidst great rejoicing, firing of guns, military bands and cheers from the Highlanders. In the years ahead, as well as passengers and sightseers, boats sailing through the Canal carried, and still carry, a lively trade between Ireland, the West of Scotland and the northern European countries, in coal, building materials, metals, chemicals, timber, oil and grain.

Part of Caledonian Canal, 1890

A Family of Lighthouse Engineers

The coastline of Scotland from the town of Berwick in the east to the Solway Firth on the west is about four thousand nautical miles, and before lighthouses were built the coast, particularly of West Scotland, was one of the most dangerous in Europe for ships.

In winter, especially when great gales blew and storms raged, the complete darkness of night struck terror into the heart of every sailor who found himself in the Scottish waters and many captains would sail their ships only in daylight. Although nowadays there are so few shipwrecks round the British coasts that they are widely reported in newspapers and on television when they do occur, it was not always so. For example in the year 1833 there were more than 800 wrecks due to storm, fog and darkness. And this was not unusual. There was a great need to light up our shores.

The idea of lighthouses was not new. In 280 BC the great lighthouse of Pharos, one of the wonders of the ancient world, was built at the entrance to the port of Alexandria in Egypt. The Romans, too, built many lighthouses around the Mediterranean Sea, but when their empire collapsed in about AD 400 many of the lessons that they had taught civilisation seemed to have been forgotten. It was not until the 16th century that a huge beacon was built at the port of Leith, near Edinburgh, to guide ships into the harbour and, in 1566, Aberdeen Town Council set up a great portable lantern consisting of three flaming oil lamps at the harbour entrance. The first lighthouse to be built in Scotland, however, was in 1636 on the Isle of May at the entrance of the Firth of Forth. Lighthouses were then being built in many parts of the world and great improvements were being made in the 300 lighting systems, by means of reflectors and revolving lights. This was the time when Scottish trade was through ports on its east coast, such as Leith, Montrose and Aberdeen, from which ships sailed to Europe. When the Union of Scotland with England came about in 1707, the West Indies and America, which had formerly been closed to Scotland, were opened up for trade and so the ports in the west of Scotland, particularly Glasgow, became the important ones. The river Clyde was deepened so that the great merchant ships from the Americas could sail right into the heart of Glasgow, which developed from being a rather sleepy little town into one of the great trading centres of the world. But the Clyde was a dangerous river and so a lighthouse was built on the Little Cumbrae island and another, called the Cloch, on the Ayrshire coast near Gourock.

Cloch Lighthouse

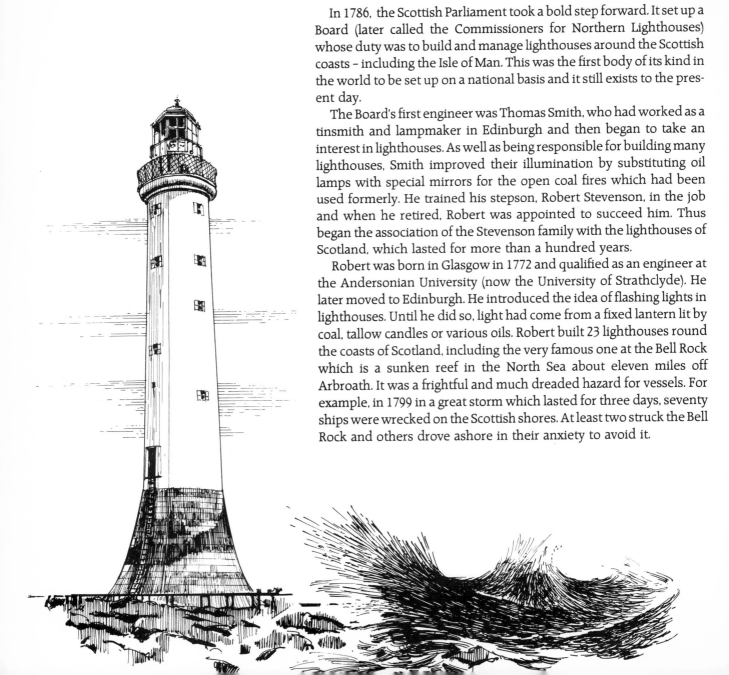

In 1786, the Scottish Parliament took a bold step forward. It set up a Board (later called the Commissioners for Northern Lighthouses) whose duty was to build and manage lighthouses around the Scottish coasts – including the Isle of Man. This was the first body of its kind in the world to be set up on a national basis and it still exists to the present day.

The Board's first engineer was Thomas Smith, who had worked as a tinsmith and lampmaker in Edinburgh and then began to take an interest in lighthouses. As well as being responsible for building many lighthouses, Smith improved their illumination by substituting oil lamps with special mirrors for the open coal fires which had been used formerly. He trained his stepson, Robert Stevenson, in the job and when he retired, Robert was appointed to succeed him. Thus began the association of the Stevenson family with the lighthouses of Scotland, which lasted for more than a hundred years.

Robert was born in Glasgow in 1772 and qualified as an engineer at the Andersonian University (now the University of Strathclyde). He later moved to Edinburgh. He introduced the idea of flashing lights in lighthouses. Until he did so, light had come from a fixed lantern lit by coal, tallow candles or various oils. Robert built 23 lighthouses round the coasts of Scotland, including the very famous one at the Bell Rock which is a sunken reef in the North Sea about eleven miles off Arbroath. It was a frightful and much dreaded hazard for vessels. For example, in 1799 in a great storm which lasted for three days, seventy ships were wrecked on the Scottish shores. At least two struck the Bell Rock and others drove ashore in their anxiety to avoid it.

From the planning stage, the lighthouse took six years (1806-1811) to build under the most difficult conditions imaginable; its construction has been described as outstanding in the history of lighthouses. The men, under Stevenson's direction, worked from a ship which was chartered for the purpose. They could work only when the Rock was exposed at low tides and when weather permitted. Heavy stones had to be brought from the mainland and the stonemasons working on the Rock were often knee-deep in water. When the six great beams – 50 feet (15 metres) long and 18 inches (45 cm) square – which would form the legs of the beacon were being placed in position, a team of more than fifty men worked with water up to their waists. Stones which had been carefully cut were now fitted in position by means of cranes and gradually the stone lighthouse took shape. Finally it was fitted with lanterns and with a bell which tolled when the weather was foggy.

Robert's second son, David, who was also an engineer, introduced the use of paraffin oil, which was produced by the great shale oil works near Bathgate. David also constructed many lighthouses not only in Britain but also in Japan. Two more of Robert's sons, Alan and Thomas, were engineers to the Board. Alan designed and built ten lighthouses, including the very famous one at Skerryvore on the island of Tiree. He was the father of the famous novelist Robert Louis Stevenson, the author of, among others, two of the most exciting adventure stories ever written – *Kidnapped* and *Treasure Island.* He also wrote a book about the work of the Stevenson family in lighthouse building. He called it *A Family of Engineers.* Thomas carried on the work that had been begun by his brother Alan and greatly improved the lighting power of lighthouses so that they gave out a more brilliant and penetrating light. The Stevenson family were responsible for great improvements in lighthouses that took place not only in Scotland, but all over the world.

Today the big ships don't need the lighthouses as much as they did because they are fitted with radar and other electronic devices that help them to pinpoint their position. Now there are 221 beacons and lights in Scotland, but only 52 of them are manned. The others have all been automated and it is only a matter of time till the remainder follow.

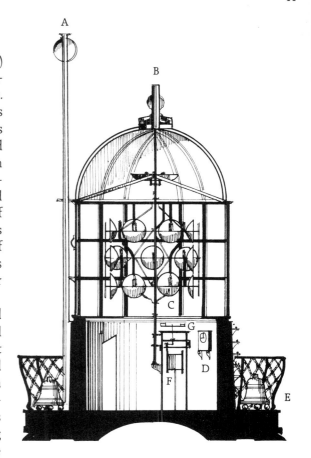

How the Bell Rock Lighthouse worked

A — Chimney

B — Vent for smoke and fumes from oil burners

C — Silvered, beaten copper parabolic reflector bowls in groups of seven, with oil flame in front of each

D — Clock

E — Fog warning bell

F — Hand-cranked gravity mechanism worked by drum and coiled rope

G — Governor arm to control speed

Railways

Less than two hundred years ago, the only way of travelling any distance in Scotland was by sea, which was very dangerous, or by stage-coach which was very expensive and very uncomfortable. The roads were rough and uneven and the stage-coach wheels were solid. So most people stayed at home in their own little towns and villages as their ancestors had done for hundreds of years before them They never moved away, not even for a visit, from the day that they were born until the day that they died.

The coming of the railways changed all that. But the early trains were not all that comfortable either. In 1850, when the Scottish and English railway systems were linked up, the Caledonian Railway ran the first excursion train from Carlisle to the Highland Show in Glasgow. This consisted of twenty cattle trucks with straw on the floor and the passengers were pushed in like sheep, having to stand up closely-packed together for the twelve-hour journey.

Trucks, pulled or pushed around on rails, had been in use in mines for a very long time. Steam carriages had also been tried out on roads, for example by the Scotsman William Murdoch in Cornwall in 1786. But it was George Stephenson, a Newcastle engineer, who first put the two together. On 27 September 1825, his engine 'Locomotion No 1' – a long train of wagons full of coal and excited passengers – travelled from Darlington to Stockton with Stephenson at the controls, at a speed of 8 mph (13 kph). He has been called the 'father of railways'. Six years later two Glasgow-built locomotives were used to carry coal from the heart of the Lanarkshire coalfields near Airdrie, to the Forth and Clyde Canal at Kirkintilloch. The coal wagons were taken straight on to the ferries and then taken by canal to the factories of Glasgow or to ocean-going ships. There were difficulties. The engines were found to be too big to pass through one of the tunnels between Airdrie and Kirkintilloch, so the roof had to be taken off the tunnel!

In 1831 the first public passenger railway in Scotland ran between Garnkirk and Glasgow – a distance of eight miles (thirteen km). Soon railways were travelling to all parts of Scotland. Their coming meant that Scotland began to develop as a great industrial nation. She had lots of coal to provide the power and the great coalfields of Lanarkshire, Ayrshire and Fife were opened up. She had lots of iron ore from

which steel could be made. She had lots of men of ability who were accustomed to hard work. Now she had the railways to carry the raw materials to the works and also to carry the finished products from the works and factories to her many busy ports, whence they could be sent all over the world.

The Industrial Revolution, although it had many dark sides, also made it possible for families to afford holidays for the first time. Small villages on the coast became flourishing holiday resorts, because people could now move about freely and cheaply. And not only on land. Soon after a railway line was established from Glasgow to Gourrock on the Clyde coast in 1841, railway companies started to have

Between about 1860 and 1920, Glasgow was probably the chief centre in the world for building railway engines. Thousands of these were exported, until it was said that Scottish-built steam locomotives were running on every railway in the world.

their own steamers. Glasgow people started sailing 'doon the watter'.

The railway line opened between Edinburgh and Glasgow in 1842 was an important one. It put an end to the stage-coach and later the Forth and Clyde Canal. The opening of the Aberdeen railway in 1850 ended the isolation of that fine city and meant that the citizens could travel, not only to Glasgow and Edinburgh, but also directly to London. Rich city merchants and businessmen realised that they and their families didn't have to live in the industrial grime and soot of the cities. They began to build their homes out in the country. So house building companies began to develop and in order to encourage rich people to buy such houses, they offered free rail travel. If you bought a £1000 house in Lenzie – about eight miles (thirteen km) from the centre of Glasgow – you could have a free season ticket on the train for ten years. Even until 1933 there was free travel from Clarkston six miles (ten km) from Glasgow.

Stephen

Smith

Fleming

Supporters could follow their football teams and the railway companies built stations near the football grounds. They even constructed golf courses with lavish hotels nearby. Turnberry and Gleneagles are two good examples.

Competition between the railway companies became intense and many small ones were not able to survive. By 1923 only two major companies (based in London) were operating trains in Scotland – the LMS (London Midland & Scottish) and the LNER (London, North Eastern Railway); their two most famous engines were the Royal Scot (LMS) and the Flying Scotsman (LNER). Although there were only two companies the steam train was still at its height. Edinburgh Waverley had 21 platforms – the largest outside London – and Glasgow Central was dealing with 22 million passengers a year.

Three Scots were among those who contributed most to the building of the Canadian Pacific Railway (1871-1875). It ran right across Canada and was the world's longest and most expensive railway. It was about 2500 miles (4000 km) long, and went across some of the most difficult territory in the world, some if it unexplored.

Sandford Fleming (1827-1915), born in Kirkcaldy, was the first person to propose a plan for building the railway, of which he became the first engineer-in-chief. To survey possible routes, he and a few companions (including a Scottish Presbyterian minister called George Grant) travelled over five thousand miles in 103 days, by whatever transport they could find, but often on foot.

Donald A. Smith (1820-1914), born in Forres, was a businessman who shared the Government's belief that a railway linking the eastern states of Canada with the state of British Columbia on the west coast was essential if the country was to be properly governed. He and his cousin George Stephen (1829-1921), who was born in Dufftown, formed a company to build it, and several times faced personal ruin as the operation ran continually into debt. It was saved finally at the last minute when the company offered to transport three thousand troops half-way across Canada in ten days in winter, to put down an Indian rebellion. They did it, although there were still four vast gaps in the line.

The Canadian Pacific Railway was built under appalling conditions across lakes, swamps, rivers and prairies, and through and over mountain ranges which were thought to be impenetrable. At several points it was required to follow the shore of Lake Superior where solid rock came right down to the edge of the water.

The Forth and Tay Bridges

Because Scotland has so many rivers cutting deep into the country, she needs bridges. It is not surprising, then, that Scotland produced many great architects and engineers who built bridges not only in Scotland, but also in England, Wales and abroad. We have already seen for example, that when Thomas Telford was building roads in the Highlands, he built over a thousand bridges there. He built the great Menai and Conway suspension bridges in Wales during the construction of a road from London to Holyhead. He was also consulted by the Austrian and British Governments on the building of roads and bridges.

Another Scot, John Rennie, built the bridges at Southwark and Westminster, both over the River Thames in London and he designed the new London Bridge which was built by his son. Robert Mylne built the bridge at Blackfriars over the Thames as well as many others.

Two of the greatest estuaries in Scotland are the Forth and the Tay and that is where four of Scotland's greatest bridges – two road and two rail – have been built.

In 1871 the first railway bridge over the River Tay was begun. When it was finished six years later, it was the longest bridge in the world. In its building, twenty lives were lost. But worse was to follow. On Sunday, 28 December 1879, a great tempest howled. Men were unable to stand upright, so great was the gale. And at seven o'clock at night, when a train was passing over, the bridge collapsed and the train with its passengers plunged into the freezing waters below. All 75 passengers lost their lives. It is said that when the builder of the bridge, Sir Thomas Bouch heard the news, his hair turned white overnight. There was an official inquiry and although the reasons for the disaster were never fully established, there was some criticism of his methods and Sir Thomas, who had got his knighthood for building the bridge, died of a broken heart four months afterwards.

A second Tay Railway Bridge was begun in 1885 to replace the one lost in the disaster of 1879. Although the old bridge had been in existence only a short time, it had proved the need for such a connection. The new bridge, 10,711 ft (3265 metres) in length is the longest railway bridge in Britain. Of this, 8396 ft (2560 metres) is in a straight line over the narrowest part of the river; it then takes a wide curve for the remainder of its length to bring it right into the station at Dundee. The bridge is built of wrought-iron and it is supported on 85 double piers made of cast-iron lined with brick and filled with concrete. Each pier is connected near the top by a semi-circular arch.

Bearing in mind what had happened to the first Tay Railway Bridge, the architects and builders asked the Railway Company about their experience of wind pressure on trains. They were told that a wind pressure of 30-40 lbs per square foot had been sufficient to overturn railway carriages. They therefore decided to build the bridge to withstand a wind pressure of 56 lb. They have proved to be correct, for no accidents have been recorded on their bridge.

There were some during its construction, however. In the five years it took to build, thirteen lives were lost. One report said that this was quite satisfactory, as the deaths were due, not to the method of construction, but to the carelessness of the men themselves! Thankfully, attitudes to the loss of life of workmen have markedly changed today.

The big increase in motor traffic in the 1950s and 1960s meant that a road bridge was needed over the River Tay from Dundee to the Fife coast. The building of the bridge began in 1963 and it was opened three and a half years later by Queen Elizabeth The Queen Mother. It was built from the Dundee side only and consists of a double line of hollow, square steel piles driven down into the bed-rock and then filled with concrete, with the concrete roadway on top. The roadway, which is 7365 ft (2245 metres) long, is the longest river crossing of any bridge in Britain. It has two double-lane carriageways. Each carriageway is 22 ft (6.7 metres) wide and between them is a central footpath, with viewing platforms arranged at intervals. If you walk along the footpath from Dundee to the Fife coast, then you are walking uphill all the way, since it rises from 32 ft (10 metres) above sea level at Dundee to 125 ft (38 metres) in Fife.

The architect, Sir William Fairhurst, realised that if the piers were all equally spaced, then they would not appear to be so to the observer from the shore. So the piers nearer to the two shores are closer together than those out in the river. The human eye tells us that they are all equally spaced.

Tay Road Bridge

Forth Railway Bridge

The Forth Railway Bridge was begun in 1883 and it took seven years to build. Lessons had been learned from the Tay disaster and it was built to withstand a wind pressure of 56 lb per square foot. This was much more than was actually required (today 30 lb is regarded as sufficient), but the designers were obviously going to err on the side of safety. The Tay railway bridge which collapsed was built to withstand a wind pressure of only 20 lb.

The structure of the bridge was new to Britain and although some people did not like the design, it has certainly been very efficient, since trains are still running on it today. Three tapered steel towers rest on small circular stone piers. Each tower supports cantilevered arms made of mild steel which balance each other on either side of the tower and linked by steel arch trusses. It was indeed the first bridge in the world to be constructed of such steel (rather than iron). Along the bridge there are twin railway tracks which are about 150 ft (45 metres) above the water. On each side of the railway there are footpaths. The whole structure, including its approaches, is 1½ miles (2.4 km) long and it was the longest bridge in the world until the Quebec Bridge over the St Lawrence River in Canada was built in 1917. Because mild steel rusts, the Forth Bridge has to be protected by paint. About 72 hectares have to be covered. It is not surprising that as soon as the job is completed the painters have to start at the beginning again.

The Forth Road Bridge is the largest suspension bridge in Europe and is the fourth largest in the world. Including its approach viaducts, it is more than 1½ miles (2.5 km) long. Until it was built, linking up Fife and the North with Edinburgh and the South, the only way across the Firth (other than by rail) was by ferries, which had a history of going back and forth of more than eight hundred years.

The bridge has two main towers – one on each side of the river. These are 512 ft (156 metres) above the river level. Work was begun on the two towers simultaneously and the bed of the River Forth had to be penetrated by underwater blasting of the rock so that the foundations of the towers could be laid.

In a suspension bridge, the whole weight of the roadway is carried by cables and in order to take this great weight, two cable anchorages, to which the ends of the cables could be secured, were built on each side of the river. Each one was made of 10,500 tons (10,650 tonnes) of

Forth Road Bridge

concrete and into the concrete were set steel tubes through which the 2 ft (60 cm) diameter cables could be passed. These anchorages could resist a pull of 14,000 tons. The cables, which had a strength of over a hundred tons per square inch, were anchored to these, hauled over the tops of the 512 ft (156 metre) towers and attached to the suspended roadway. The cables contained enough wire to stretch $1\frac{1}{4}$ times round the Equator.

On 20 December 1963, the watching spectators saw a very dramatic sight. The two parts of the suspended steelwork carrying the roadway – one part from the Edinburgh side and one part from the Fife side – met halfway across the estuary and were fixed together. They were no more than an inch out. Thus the Forth Road Bridge was completed.

The roadway consists of a double carriage-way each 24 ft (7 metres) wide and designed to carry the heaviest loading permitted on any bridge in the world, including vehicles weighing up to 180 tonnes. In addition there are two cycle tracks, each 9 ft (2.5 metres) wide and two footpaths each 6 ft (2 metres) wide.

Great Liners

The Act of Union between England and Scotland in 1707 meant that trade with the Americas was now open to Scotland. The ports on the west coast of Scotland became very important, particularly those in the great estuary of the Clyde into which the merchant sailing ships sailed. But this did not help Glasgow much, because the Clyde was so shallow (only 16 inches — 40 cm deep at Glasgow) that the ships could only sail as far as Greenock, where they unloaded. The Glasgow merchants were very concerned so they established their own port – Port Glasgow. But this was still 10 miles (16 km) from Glasgow and the goods had to be brought up from there in flat bottomed barges at high water. Sometimes they were stuck on the sandbanks for weeks.

There was only one remedy. The river Clyde would have to be deepened up to Glasgow. In 1768 the magistrates asked John Golborne, an engineer from Chester, to solve the problem. He did so by using two methods. He built wooden jetties out into the river so that the channel became a very narrow one: and small boats dragged large rakes along the bottom of the channel between the jetties. By the time he had finished in 1775 he had deepened the Clyde even more than he had said he would and the Glasgow magistrates paid him an extra £1500 and gave him a silver cup. Merchant ships could now sail right into the heart of Glasgow. Ever since then the channel has been regularly dredged so that it is now about 30 ft (9 m) deeper than it was originally.

In 1812 Henry Bell launched on the Clyde the 'Comet', the first steamship to carry on a regular passenger service in any European river. Although the 'Comet' sank in 1820, there were soon plenty more to take her place. Henry Bell had begun a new era and the Clyde was to become famous for her steamships.

Samuel Cunard, a Canadian, founded the Cunard Shipping Company in 1839 with the purpose of establishing and maintaining a regular steamer service across the Atlantic and his company built many ships in Clyde shipyards. The 'Britannia' built at Greenock in 1840, was a wooden paddle steamer with three large masts. She took 12 days and 10 hours to sail from Liverpool to Halifax at a speed of $8\frac{1}{2}$ knots, burning 38 tons of coal per day. It is interesting to note that she carried

Dredging the Clyde

cows in a special 'cow-house' to provide fresh milk, because there was no refrigeration in those days.

Ships built of iron and a little later of steel were soon to replace wooden ships. Glasgow and neighbouring districts were well placed to take advantage of this development for their iron and steel works were already famous. The first steel Cunarder 'Service' built in Clydebank in 1880 won the Blue Riband as the fastest ship on the Atlantic run. The 'Virginian' which was built by Alexander Stephen, Glasgow in 1905 for the Allen Line, was the first turbine driven steamship and could reach the east coast of Canada in just six days.

One of the most tragic ships was the 'Lusitania', built in John Brown's shipyards, Clydebank in 1907. Her 25 boilers and 192 furnaces consumed a thousand tons of coal a day. She was a magnificently fitted ship of over 31,000 tons and could carry over two thousand passengers. She was torpedoed and sunk by the German Navy off the Irish coast in 1915. Most of the crew and passengers were drowned, including a number of Americans and this was said to be a major factor in bringing America into the War.

By the outbreak of World War I in 1914 the Clyde shipyards were building about half of the world's tonnage and employing about 100,000 workmen.

The pride of the Cunard fleet were the 'Queens'. The 'Queen Mary' of over 80,000 tons, the world's largest ship of the time, was built in John Brown's. Work began in 1930, but a year later depression reached the Clyde: building was halted and was not resumed till 1934. She was launched by Queen Mary, the wife of King George V. The 140-ton rudder had a door in its side so that it could be inspected internally in dry dock. The anchors weighed sixteen tons each. Ten million rivets were used in building the ship and she had 257,000 turbine blades. Even the three whistles weighed one ton each and could be heard for ten miles. She captured the Blue Riband with a run which averaged 31.6 knots.

The Cunard dream was that they should have a sister ship for the 'Queen Mary' so the 'Queen Elizabeth' was begun in John Brown's shipyard in 1936. Construction was given priority and the shipyard worked round the clock, aided by great floodlights. Like her famous 'sister' she was over 80,000 tons in weight. Her Majesty Queen Mary

Lusitania

The building of a great liner is a long and complicated business. The desired tonnage and speed of the ship are given to the designer. He knows the depth of water of the harbours into which the ship will sail and so he calculates the design of the ship.

Models of the ship are built and tested out in special tanks in which waves are artificially created. When the final design is determined, drawings and plans are made. From them full size wooden or paper patterns, on which are marked all the places for rivets, are constructed for each piece of steel that will be used in building the ship. The patterns are fitted over the steel plate and all the rivet holes are punched out.

In the meantime the keel of the ship is laid down near the river. The steel plates are then riveted on to it like large overlapping fish scales. So the outside steel shell of the ship is completed.

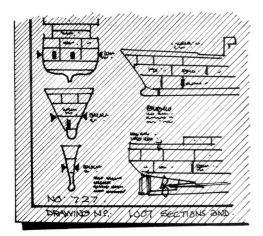

Then the engine rooms are fitted out. Modern ships have a false bottom to lessen the damage if the hull should be pierced on a voyage. The hull is also divided into water-tight compartments. Remember that when the 'Queens' were built, the designers had no computer to help them with their calculations. It hadn't been invented.

the Queen Mother named her, but it is said that the ship began to move before she began her speech. She had the presence of mind to release the bottle of champagne quickly! As World War II loomed, many workers were taken off the QE and put to work on naval ships. A proposal was made that she should be sold to the USA but this was turned down. Instead, in 1940, the unfinished ship sailed for New York to join the 'Queen Mary' and, like her, to be fitted out as a troop carrier. Winston Churchill, the war-time Prime Minister, said that these two ships alone shortened the war in Europe by a year by transporting over 1½ million troops and eleven million tons of cargo between the USA and Britain. When the war was over the two 'Queens' resumed their Atlantic run as passenger ships, but by the 1960s the jet aircraft was making its appearance and the days of transatlantic travel by sea were numbered. The 'Queen Mary' was sold to Long Beach, California in 1967 and was turned into a museum – hotel – convention centre.

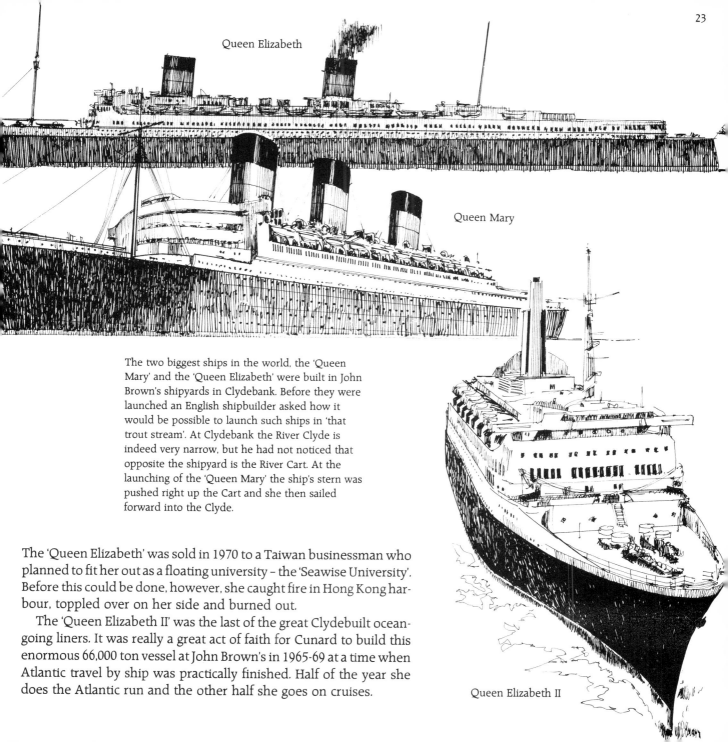

Queen Elizabeth

Queen Mary

The two biggest ships in the world, the 'Queen Mary' and the 'Queen Elizabeth' were built in John Brown's shipyards in Clydebank. Before they were launched an English shipbuilder asked how it would be possible to launch such ships in 'that trout stream'. At Clydebank the River Clyde is indeed very narrow, but he had not noticed that opposite the shipyard is the River Cart. At the launching of the 'Queen Mary' the ship's stern was pushed right up the Cart and she then sailed forward into the Clyde.

The 'Queen Elizabeth' was sold in 1970 to a Taiwan businessman who planned to fit her out as a floating university – the 'Seawise University'. Before this could be done, however, she caught fire in Hong Kong harbour, toppled over on her side and burned out.

The 'Queen Elizabeth II' was the last of the great Clydebuilt ocean-going liners. It was really a great act of faith for Cunard to build this enormous 66,000 ton vessel at John Brown's in 1965-69 at a time when Atlantic travel by ship was practically finished. Half of the year she does the Atlantic run and the other half she goes on cruises.

Queen Elizabeth II

Three famous Architects

Robert Adam (1728-1792) was a very lucky man. When he was only a boy, his father gave him a ruined castle as a birthday present. He decided to be an architect like his father. He went to school in Kirkcaldy, then on to the High School in Edinburgh and so to study at Edinburgh University. The Adam family was fairly wealthy so Robert was able to spend three years in Italy, mainly in Rome, where, in addition to enjoying himself, he was able to study with some of the great architects of the time. When he returned to England he set up in business with his brother James. The business thrived, for not only was Robert a brilliant architect, but he had many influential friends. Soon he was building great homes all over England and he was made one of His Majesty's architects

Adam took a personal interest in every aspect of the building that he was creating and he insisted on the highest standards, both for the outside and the inside. He even supervised the making of the curtains and the candle snuffers. He employed only the best firms – Chippendale to make the furniture and the famous pottery makers Wedgwood to make the tea and dinner services. His ceilings and fireplaces were famous so that even today one can instantly recognise them. He wrote books on architecture, too, and for a short time he was a Member of Parliament.

At the time of his death, Adam was involved in eight public and 25 private buildings, having also found time to design the beautiful Charlotte Square in Edinburgh. With Dukes and Earls carrying his coffin, he was buried in Westminster Abbey.

Robert Mylne (1734-1811) was a young Scottish architect who studied in Italy at the same time as Robert Adam. He was also of a wealthy family and his father, too, an architect. While in Rome he won first prize in an international competition. When he returned to Britain he entered another competition – for the design of a bridge over the Thames at Blackfriars. He went on to build the bridge. He built many bridges including one over the River Clyde and one over the River Tyne, and several in the grounds of Warwick Castle; he designed docks and reservoirs and hospitals. And he worked for the Duke of Argyll on both the town of Inveraray and Inveraray Castle.

He was appointed architect to the City of London and surveyor to

One of Adam's most famous buildings is Culzean Castle, on the Ayrshire coast near Girvan. He was asked by the owner, the Earl of Cassilis, to reconstruct the old house there, and to enlarge it, which he did by building two great blocks on each side. In ten years Adam created a magnificent castle which stands high on a rock, projecting out to sea. Inside, the rooms are beautifully decorated and furnished including an armoury with 40 pistols arranged in a circle around the clock; a library with a set of Chippendale chairs; a dining-room lit by a magnificent chandelier fitted out for gas lighting and a 16 ft dining table set out with a Wedgwood dinner service. An imposing staircase leads to the long drawing-room with its beautiful ceiling and ornamental mirror and so to the Green drawing-room whose furnishings are French; and finally the bedrooms. In 1946 the top floor of the main part of the house was converted as a separate flat and put at the disposal of General Dwight D. Eisenhower during his lifetime as a token of gratitude for the work that he had done as Supreme Commander of the Allied Forces in Europe during World War II.

Canterbury Cathedral, St Paul's Cathedral and the Abbey Church of St Albans. He was responsible for arranging public ceremonies in the City and he made the arrangements for the funeral of Admiral Lord Nelson.

Charles Rennie Mackintosh (1868-1923) has been described as the greatest Scottish architect since Adam. And yet, strangely enough, until recently his work was not greatly appreciated in Scotland and some of the buildings that he designed in Glasgow have been demolished. In Europe, however, his importance as an architect was recognised early.

Mackintosh was born in Glasgow in 1868. After leaving school he joined a firm of architects and attended evening classes at the Glasgow Art School. He won many prizes there, including a scholarship which allowed him to study for a short time in Italy. In 1895, when the School required a new building, it was he who won the competition for its design.

In 1896 he was introduced to a lady, Kate Cranston, who commissioned him to design and supervise the building and decoration of three tea-rooms for her in Glasgow. Unfortunately they have all gone, although the 'Willow' in Sauchiehall Street (the name Sauchiehall means 'alley of willows') has been restored to much of its former beauty and is now a jewellers shop. He also designed the Hill House in Helensburgh for Walter Blackie, the publisher. It is now a Mackintosh museum.

When Mackintosh designed a house or tea-room he also designed the furniture, carpets, curtains, clocks and cutlery. Mackintosh's work was far ahead of his time. It was described as 'avant-garde'.

The Glasgow Underground

The job of construction was a difficult and dangerous one and it is a great tribute to the engineering skills of the Company that no lives were lost during its construction, though there were plenty of scares and alarms due to flooding, fire and subsidence.

When the Glasgow District Subway Company announced in a small newspaper advertisement that a newly-constructed underground railway (the Subway) would be open to the public on Monday, 14 December 1896, they did not anticipate the rush that there would be to use it. Before 8 am all fifteen stations were besieged. It was not surprising, perhaps, that so many people came along. Above, the gloomy gas-lit streets of Victorian Glasgow were jammed with carters and horse-drawn trams – and it was cold. Below ground, the warm, electrically-lighted cars sped at 13 mph from station to station every three minutes between 6.30 am and 11 pm. They took only 28 minutes to complete the 6½ miles (10.5 km) circuit. They have been doing more or less the same right down to the present day.

The underground railway took about 4½ years to build and it was done by opening up the streets at certain points, excavating, and then linking up the various excavations. In this way 6½ miles (10.5 km) of two cylindrical tubes, or tunnels, each 11 ft (3.5 m) in diameter were constructed side by side (the so-called 'outer' and 'inner' circles).

The original cars were beautifully constructed with the doors, ends and partitions of polished teak with panels of oak and the roof bearings of white ash wood. Many of them were still in use in 1974.

Hillhead Station in about 1970

The underground staff were, perhaps not surprisingly, known as 'moles'. Each two-car train had a staff of three – a 'gripman' who was the driver, a conductor who issued tickets and a 'smokeboy' or assistant conductor (paid 45p a week) who collected the tickets as the passengers alighted. The hours were long for all of them – they worked seven days a week with no time off for meals, but there were 'perks' – the Company gave them a house at a cheap rent. The uniforms were simple in most cases, but the Chief Inspector who was stationed at Hillhead, wore a gold-braided cap and brown uniform frock-coat. When Queen Victoria died in 1901 all inspectors had black braid woven into their cuffs. This black braid remained part of the official uniform until 1974.

In 1922, the ownership of the Subway (or Underground as it came to be officially known) was taken over by Glasgow Corporation and in 1933 the cable system was replaced by electric rails and the cars were fitted with old tramway engines. As the years went on, however, it became more difficult and more expensive to replace worn-out parts and a complete renewal was begun in 1977. By the time the Queen opened the refitted Underground in 1979, all that was left of the old were the two tunnels. The stations were modernised and some were renamed. Escalators replaced the steps in the 'deep' stations such as Buchanan Street and Hillhead; and new trains ran on new rails. So, as the new system appeared the old vanished into the past. Well, not completely. When word got around that it was to be modernised, more than 22 film and television teams came and recorded, for all time, the subway that had been loved by so many.

The cars were run on cable systems. The source of power – the power house in Scotland St – consisted of eight huge boilers which supplied steam to a pair of enormous stationary steam engines – one for each circle. Pulleys and driving shafts transferred power from engines to cables. Each of the cables weighed 57 tons measured nearly seven miles (eleven km) long and ran at a constant speed of 13 mph (21 kph).

Hydroelectric Power

In 1831 Michael Faraday showed that if a moving magnet was rotated inside a coil of wire then electricity was generated and moved along the wires. Fifty years later, in 1882, Thomas Edison, using steam power to rotate magnets, supplied electric light to a number of homes in New York. The same principal is still used today to generate electricity, the power being supplied by steam produced by water heated by coal, oil, gas or nuclear power. An exception, however, is *hydropower* where the generators are powered not by steam, but by running water.

The use of water power in Scotland goes back to at least the 12th century. Early factories were built near rivers where the running water turned wooden paddles, which provided power for the production of flour, paper, textiles or the cutting of tree trunks into logs. It was only, however, after Thomas Edison showed in 1831 that mechanical energy could be turned into electrical energy that thought was given to using the mechanical energy provided by running water to provide an electricity supply.

The first public supply of electricity by hydro power was installed near the St Benedictine Abbey in Fort Augustus in 1890. It remained in operation until 1951. In the years that followed, a number of private companies set up stations. The major development was, however, the establishment of the North of Scotland Hydro-Electric Board in 1943. Its responsibility was to produce and distribute electricity to an area north and west of a line joining the Firth of Clyde and the Firth of Tay including all the islands, extending to the Outer Hebrides, Orkneys and Shetlands. This is two-thirds of the area of Scotland. At that time only one farm in six and one croft in a hundred had electricity. The others were lit by oil lamps and candles.

Between 1945, when construction work began, and the mid 1960s when most of the construction work was over, the Board had built 56 major dams; 54 power stations; and two hundred miles (320 km) of rock tunnel had been excavated and pipelines laid. There were 20,000 miles (over 32,000 km) of overhead cable laid across the countryside and seventy miles (112 km) of submarine cable laid to connect up the islands. In addition they had constructed four hundred miles (650 km) of roads and built five hundred houses. They were, and still are providing electricity to half a million customers though not all of it is from hydro power. 99% of all potential customers are now connected into the system. Much of the Highlands and Islands took the huge leap from oil lamps to electricity. And during the period of construction the Board were providing work for five thousand people.

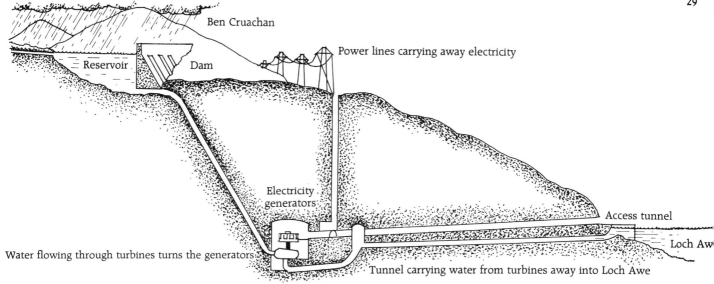

Ben Cruachan

Power lines carrying away electricity

Reservoir

Dam

Electricity generators

Access tunnel

Loch Aw[e]

Water flowing through turbines turns the generators.

Tunnel carrying water from turbines away into Loch Awe

The first scheme was at Loch Sloy which lies in the hills 935 ft (285 metres) above sea-level, where the average rainfall is over 120 ins (3000 mm) a year. More water from surrounding areas was diverted into the loch. It was doubled in length and had its surface level raised 155 ft (47 metres) by the construction of a huge dam, 182 ft (56 metres) high and 1170 ft (357 metres) long. From Loch Sloy the water is carried by pipes through Ben Vorlich to the power station at Inveruglas Bay on Loch Lomondside where it generates 120 million units of electricity per year. (1 unit = 1 kilowatt hour.) All of the hydro schemes together produce about 3 billion units per year.

The great advantages of hydro-electricity are (1) it is cheap to produce since no coal or oil is used; (2) it can supply electricity immediately it is switched on and (3) the water can be easily stored until it is required.

Although some people worried that the building of huge power stations and dams would deface the countryside and interfere with fish such as salmon, this has not proved to be so. Some of the power stations have been built *inside* mountains and some, with their dams, have great architectural beauty. Great efforts have been made to conserve salmon and other fish. In some dams, 'ladders' have been built to enable salmon and sea-trout to move upstream to spawn and a number have 'lifts' to carry fish from lower to higher levels.

In order to make electricity from water power, a dam has to be built across the end of a valley to make a reservoir. The reservoir must be fed with water not only by rain, but also by rivers and streams which run into it. A tunnel is dug down through the hillside to take the water from the reservoir down to the power station where it pushes the blades of a turbine round. As the water passes through, it is piped into a loch. Fitted to the top of the turbine is a generator. The rotor inside the generator is kept revolving by a shaft from the turbine. This generates electricity which is fed along wires which are carried across the countryside on huge pylons. When the wires reach towns they go underground to carry electricity to our homes, schools and factories.

A number of schemes e.g. at Cruachan on Loch Aweside have got what is called 'pumped storage'. At night and at week-ends, when factories are closed, there is electricity to spare which is not being used. This 'off-peak' electricity is used to pump water from Loch Awe to a reservoir high up on Ben Cruachan. This stored water is then released to generate electricity during times when it is most required.

North Sea Gas and Oil

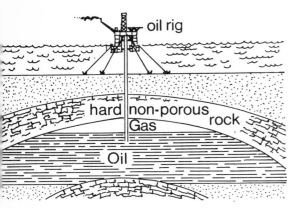

In the North Sea area the weather can be appalling. Some of the oil fields lie below almost 600 ft (180 metres) of water.

Without oil our modern society could not function. It provides fuel for our cars, lorries, aeroplanes and ships. It provides power for our factories and is turned into electricity by our power stations; it heats our homes. It is the raw material of nylon and the wide array of plastics that we know today. It can yield a whole range of chemicals including fertilisers to grow our crops and pesticides to kill our weed and insect enemies. Between them, gas and oil provide more than 70% of the world's energy.

Long ago, much of the Earth's surface was covered by oceans in which tiny animals and plants lived. As they died, their bodies sank into the sands on the ocean floor. This continued for millions of years. In certain areas these sands, or *sedimentary basins*, became trapped probably by layers of liquid rock that welled up from the centre of the Earth and flowed over them. As these rocks hardened and became thicker, great pressure was exerted on the sedimentary basins. This caused the temperature to rise about 200°C. The combined heat and pressure turned the plant and animal remains into gas and oil.

The discovery in 1959 of the huge Groningen gas fields off the Dutch coast, turned the thoughts of the oil companies to looking for more gas in the North Sea. Within a few years great gas reserves had been found off the north coast of England. The gas was piped ashore and now supplies practically all of Britain's needs for heating and lighting in homes, factories, schools and hospitals. There should be enough gas for the next thirty years.

It was while searching for more gas fields in 1969 that the rig 'Sea Quest', which was being used by the Amoco Oil Company, struck *oil* in the North Sea about 150 miles east of Aberdeen. This came as a great surprise and the first samples had to be collected in an empty pickle jar that was brought up from the galley! This find was called the Montrose Field. Others soon followed, and explorations are still going on.

It was very expensive to develop oil production in the North Sea. Cheap oil could be brought by tankers from the Middle East where the oil wells were all on land. Nevertheless, in 1971, British Petroleum decided to begin tapping a basin covering an area of about 35 square miles, which contained nearly two billion barrels of oil. Their enter-

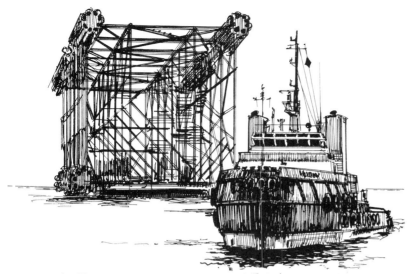

In the search for oil, a floating oil rig is positioned over the oil field. A drill is pushed down to the sea bed and deep into the rock below. The tip of the drill has rotating teeth made either of diamonds or of very hard steel which enable it to bite into the rock. During drilling a fluid known as 'mud', made up of clay, water and chemicals, is pumped down the hollow centre of the drilling pipe. This comes out through holes in the bit and is pumped up again carrying samples of rock with it. Scientists examine these rock fragments and are able to determine if oil is present.

Once it has been decided to go ahead with oil recovery, then the rig moves on and is replaced by a Production Platform. When built (which may take 1700 men two years), the jacket, which is the steel support for the platform, is towed out to sea and put in position. The raft on which it is carried is gradually filled with water. The jacket tilts over and is carefully lowered on to the sea bed. The jacket is fixed to the sea bed by great steel piles. A pre-fabricated deck module to house the crew and the equipment is then fitted to the top of the jacket.

The first job of the platform is to drill production wells. These are made in the same way as on the rig, but 40-50 bore holes are made, slanting out from the platform. Thus one platform can gather oil from a wide area. The flow of oil is regulated by a group of pipes, taps and valves called a 'Christmas Tree' — because it looks like one. Special equipment is used to remove any water and gas in the oil. Often the excess gas is burned off in a huge 'flare'.

prise paid off, when two years later the oil producing nations in the Middle East increased the price of their oil five-fold.

Today there are more than twenty off-shore oilfields run by various companies in production in the North Sea, producing about 750 million barrels of oil per year. There is a major oil terminal at Nigg Bay, but the biggest oil terminal in the world is at Sullom Voe which is on the northern shore of the mainland of Shetland. It is capable of handling 1.5 million barrels of crude oil every day.

Often oil is brought ashore to the refineries by underwater pipelines. The route is surveyed by divers and submarines. Lengths of steel pipe, surrounded by fibreglass and enamel and coated with concrete, are welded together and lowered from a barge into the water. Trenching barges bury the pipe beneath the sea bed. Divers make regular checks on the pipes. Equal care is taken with the laying of pipelines across country and to ensure that there is no destruction of the environment.

Places to Visit

Museum of Transport, Albert Drive, Glasgow, includes locomotives, reconstruction of a Subway station, original Subway coaches and fittings, ship models and a display on ship building, especially on the Clyde. The Museum will probably close for some time in 1987, in preparation for its move to Kelvin Hall, Glasgow. For information, ring 041-334 1134.

Acknowledgments

I am especially grateful to my wife Elizabeth and to my editor Antony Kamm for their practical help and encouragement. My thanks are also due to: British Waterways Board, Glasgow; Britoil, Glasgow; Mitchell Library, Glasgow; North of Scotland Hydro Electric Board, Edinburgh.

Bill Fletcher